irish humour

© the celtic quill

I LIKE PERSONS
BETTER THAN
PRINCIPLES AND
I LIKE PERSONS
WITH NO PRINCIPLES
BETTER THAN ANYTHING
ELSE IN THE WORLD.

OSCAR WILDE

The trouble
with her
is that she
lacks the power of
conversation but not
the power of speech.

G B Shaw

I can always guarantee that the Irish Citizen Army will fight, but I cannot guarantee that it will be on time.

JAMES CONNOLLY

LIKE HEARING
MYSELF TALK.
IT IS ONE OF MY
GREATEST PLEASURES.
I OFTEN HAVE LONG
CONVERSATIONS ALL BY
MYSELF, AND I AM SO
CLEVER THAT SOMETIMES
I DON'T UNDERSTAND
A SINGLE WORD OF
WHAT I AM SAYING.

OSCAR WILDE

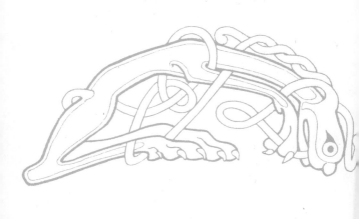

A LITTLE SINCERITY
is a dangerous thing,
and a great deal of it
is absolutely fatal.

OSCAR WILDE

A man
should have
one woman to
prevent him
from thinking
too much about
women in general.

G B SHAW

You wouldn't
worry about
what people think
if you knew how
seldom they do.

irish humour

Soft words
butter no
parsnips
but they won't
harden the heart
of a cabbage
either.

Irish proverb

When i was young i thought that money was the most important thing in life. now that i am old i know that it is.

OSCAR WILDE

WALTER
Shandy
ATTRIBUTED MOST OF
his son's misfortunes
to the fact that at a
highly critical moment,
his wife asked him if
he had wound the clock,
a question so irrelevant
that he despaired of the
child ever being able
to persue a logical
train of thought.

LAURENCE STERNE

Consistency is the last refuge of the unimaginative.

OSCAR WILDE

have been
in very good
company where
your health has
been often drank,
so that i may
say that i am
dead drunk for
your sake.

RICHARD STEELE
said to his wife

He knows
nothing and
he thinks he knows
everything; that
points clearly to
a political career.

G B Shaw

My will contains directions for my funeral, which will be followed not by mourning coaches but by herds of oxen, sheep, swine, poultry and fish, all wearing white scarves in honour of the man who perished rather than eat his fellow creatures.

G B Shaw

I'm not in favour of
long engagements;
they give people
the opportunity
of finding out
eachothers character
before marriage which
i think is never
advisable.

OSCAR WILDE

Women would
drive you mad
but the asylum
would be a
lonely place
without them.

irish humour

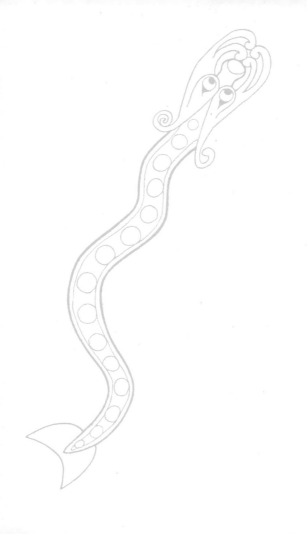

ORGIVE
YOUR ENEMIES;
NOTHING ANNOYS
THEM SO MUCH.

OSCAR WILDE

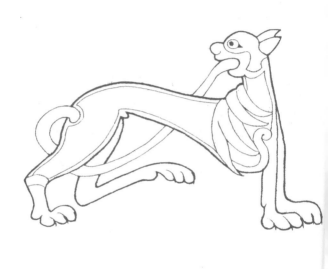

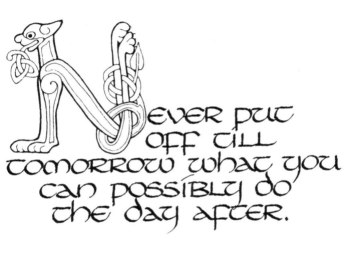

Never put off till tomorrow what you can possibly do the day after.

OSCAR WILDE

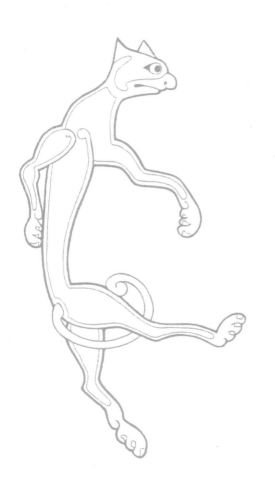

You may
certainly
not kiss the hand
that wrote Ulysses;
it's done a lot of
other things as well.

James Joyce
said to an admirer

You may
certainly
not kiss the hand
that wrote Ulysses;
it's done a lot of
other things as well.

James Joyce
said to an admirer

IRELAND IS THE ONLY COUNTRY IN THE WORLD WHERE PROCRASTINATION TAKES ON A SENSE OF URGENCY.

irish humour

Ireland is the only country in the world where procrastination takes on a sense of urgency.

irish humour

The only
thing to
do with
good advice is to
pass it on; it is
never of any use
to oneself.

OSCAR WILDE

Whenever
people
talk to me
about the weather,
i always feel certain
that they mean
something else.

oscar wilde

The thought
of two
thousand people
crunching celery
at the same time
horrified me.

G B Shaw
Refusing an invitation
to a vegetarian dinner

y duty
is a
thing i never do,
on principle.

oscar wilde

 hat the difference between a man and a woman is I cannot conceive.

John P. Mahaffy

Life is much
too important
a thing ever
to talk seriously
about it.

OSCAR WILDE

GREATER LOVE
THAN THIS, HE
SAID, NO MAN
HATH, THAT A
MAN LAY DOWN HIS
WIFE FOR HIS FRIEND.

JAMES JOYCE

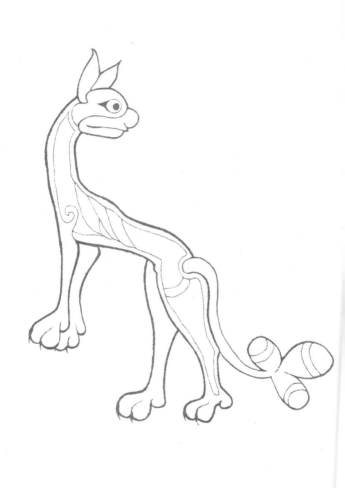

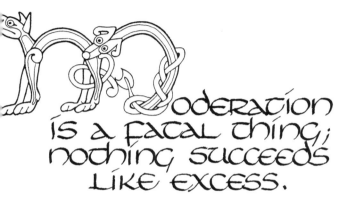

Moderation
is a fatal thing;
nothing succeeds
like excess.

OSCAR WILDE

Next to me I noticed a tall man seated, his blue eyes were fixed like all Irish eyes on futurity; I said 'it is extraordinary weather for this time of year', and he replied 'ah, it isn't this time of year at all.'

OLIVER ST JOHN GOGARTY

very saint
has a past
and every
sinner
has a future.

OSCAR WILDE

There is no satisfaction in hanging a man who does not object to it.

G B Shaw

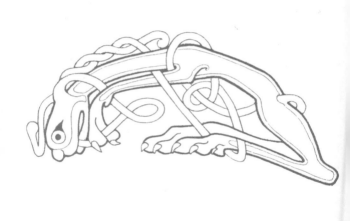

God created
whiskey
to keep
the irish from
ruling the world.

irish humour

No woman should ever be quite accurate about her age, it looks so calculating.

G B Shaw

Alfred hitchcock said that just by looking at Shaw he knew there was still famine in Ireland. Shaw replied, 'one look at you, Mr hitchcock and I know who caused it.'

Irish humour

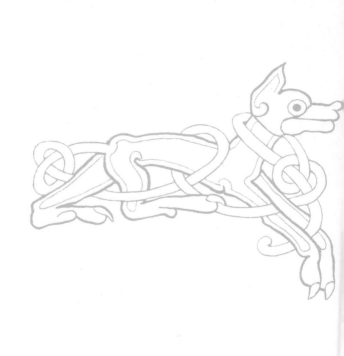

MEN CAN
BE ANALYSED,
WOMEN MERELY
ADORED.

OSCAR WILDE

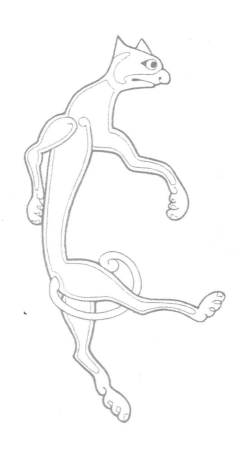

I WAS BLUE
MOULDY FOR
THE WANT OF THAT
PINT. DECLARE TO GOD,
I COULD HEAR IT
HIT THE PIT OF MY
STOMACH WITH
A CLICK.

JAMES JOYCE

I never travel without my diary; one should always have something sensational to read on the train.

OSCAR WILDE

I NEVER TRAVEL
WITHOUT MY DIARY;
ONE SHOULD ALWAYS
HAVE SOMETHING
SENSATIONAL TO
READ ON THE TRAIN.

OSCAR WILDE

e had seven
sons and had
never lifted a hand
to one except
in self defence.

irish humour

He had seven sons and had never lifted a hand to one except in self defence.

irish humour

Action is
the last
resort of people
who don't know
how to dream.

oscar wilde

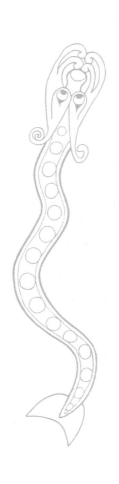

It is absurd to
divide people
into good and bad;
people are either
charming or tedious.

oscar wilde

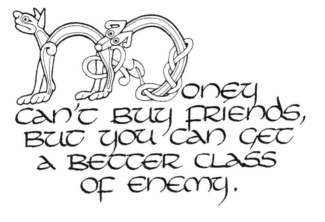

Money can't buy friends, but you can get a better class of enemy.

Irish humour

The only
way to
get rid of a
temptation is
to yield to it.

oscar wilde

WE ARE
SO FOND
OF ONE ANOTHER
BECAUSE OUR AILMENTS
ARE THE SAME.

JONATHAN SWIFT

The world is a stage
but the play is
badly cast.

Oscar Wilde

The smartest
person we
know is the
one who asks
our advice.

irish humour

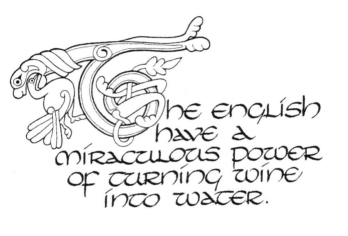

The english have a miraculous power of turning wine into water.

OSCAR WILDE

I'VE BEEN
OFFERED TITLES
BUT I THINK THEY
GET ONE INTO
DISREPUTABLE
COMPANY.

G B SHAW

The english churchgoer prefers a severe preacher, because he thinks a few home truths will do his neighbour no harm.

G B Shaw

Changeable women are more endurable than monotonous ones; they are sometimes murdered but seldom deserted.

G B Shaw

The irish
people do
not gladly suffer
common sense.

OLIVER ST JOHN GOGARTY

compilation
and design
BY
B.LENDARO
©THE CELTIC QUILL

Greann
na
héireann